GW01465401

Farming

by Peter Rice
illustrated by the author

Published for the National Trust by Dinosaur Publications

Dinosaur Publications Ltd, Over, Cambridge
The National Trust, 42 Queen Anne's Gate, London SW1

The way farming is practised in Britain varies according to the nature of the land. Hill farms have traditionally specialised in rearing beef stock as there is no shortage of water, and mountain grass suits cattle. Sheep also do well in the hills and dales and on chalk downs. Most of these areas occur in the North and West. Dairy farms need rich pastures for the cows, so the lush grass from the heavy clay areas of the Midlands and the South East is ideal. The eastern parts of England tend to be the flattest and driest and these suit arable farming.

In the hilly areas, farmers have difficulty in growing enough crops to feed their animals during the winter. Often animals are reared there and fattened somewhere else, sometimes in arable grazing areas where there is animal food to spare. In return, the manure provided by the livestock enriches the soil.

Barley   Wheat   Barley

Rye

Oats

Mustard

Clover

Crops

Each year fields are sown with different seeds so that the soil will not become exhausted. This is called crop rotation. In medieval times there was a three crop rotation; wheat first, followed by barley and then oats. During the fourth season the land was allowed to lie fallow without a crop. In the eighteenth century the Norfolk system was invented, which consisted of wheat, then roots, then barley, and in the fourth year clover and grasses. Cattle ate the grasses and manured the land. Afterwards the manure was ploughed in to enrich the wheat crop. The same systems are sometimes followed today.

The main crops grown in Britain are: cereals or grain, potatoes, sugar beet, vegetables, clovers, fodder for livestock and grass as a crop.

In livestock farming areas, most of the arable crops are used for feeding the animals. Barley is the largest crop in Britain. It is used for animal food and brewing beer. Wheat is grown mainly in the East, and only about half is used for human consumption. More oats than wheat are sown in Scotland.

The combine harvester

Wheat is generally sown in October and November and
harvested in late Summer. The corn used to be cut, tied in
bundles called sheaves, stacked and threshed. Most farms now
use a combine harvester machine which can do all these things
at once.

The mower at the front of the machine cuts the corn. The grain is then separated from the straw and carried on a conveyor belt to the threshing drum. Afterwards it is sent to the storage tank and it is unloaded through a long arm into carts and trailers. The grain is then dried. Straw and chaff is collected by the pick-up baler, which ties it up into rectangular bales.

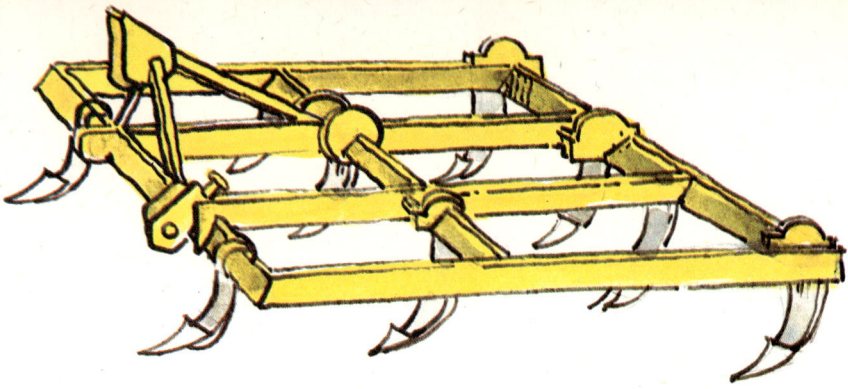

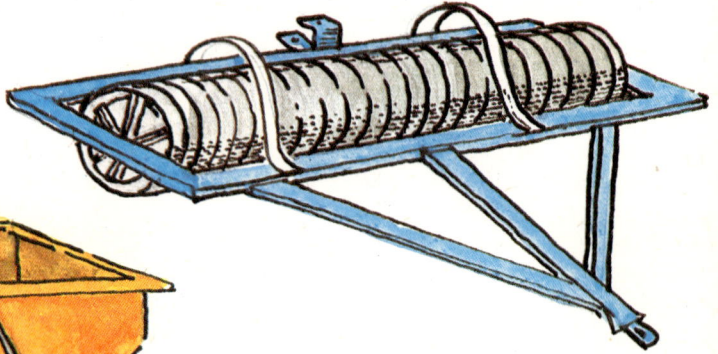

Farm Machinery

On the opposite page you can see a chisel plough. This makes furrows without turning over the earth.

Beneath it is a Cambridge roller. The ground is rolled after it has been seeded. Next to it is a fertiliser spreader.

The tractor at the bottom of the page is pulling a seed drill.

The machine at the bottom of this page is a forage harvester for cutting and collecting greens and clover for making into silage.

This plough cuts four furrows. The soil is cut vertically by round discs called coulters, and horizontally by curved metal shares.

A multi-level elevator is used for loading. Here it has been used to stack straw bales on to a lorry.

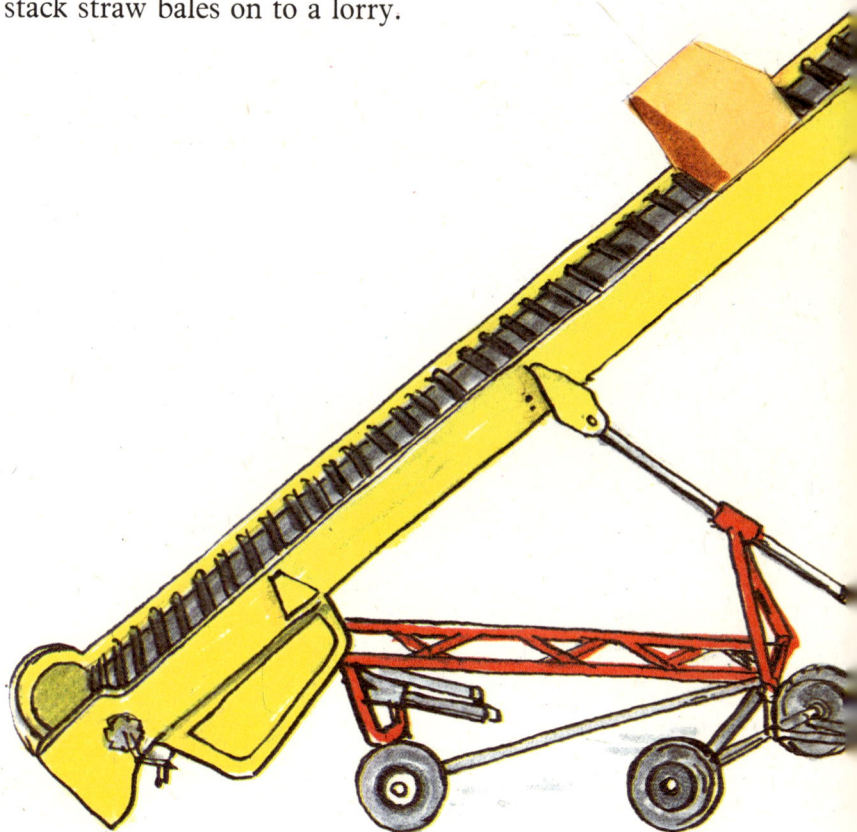

After the earth has been ploughed, it is broken up still further by the disc-harrow; after that the ground is ready for sowing seed.

Old granary on straddle stones

A battery unit for poultry

Threshing barn

Dutch barn

Dairy Breeds

Friesian

Jersey

Beef Breeds

Hereford

Aberdeen Angus

The Dairy Ring

The auctioneer is accepting bids for this cow with her calf.
Animals are bought and sold at markets, beef in the Bull Ring
and cows in the Dairy Ring.

Beef Cattle

Charolais:
A French breed introduced
in 1961. Originally it was an
all-purpose breed. Now it has
been developed as a beef
breed.

Simmenthal:
Another continental breed
recently introduced, very
docile. Nearly as large as the
Sussex, it is brown with a
white face.

Sussex:
One of the largest of British
breeds. Oxen were used as
draught animals until modern
times. It is coloured a deep
red.

Galloway:
A tough Highland breed from
Scotland with a dark woolly
coat. It is very well suited to
hill country. A variation of the
breed is the 'belted' Galloway,
which has a white stripe down
its middle.

Dairy Cattle

Dairy Shorthorn:
A popular breed from the
North East, as is the Beef
Shorthorn. There is also a
Scottish type.

Ayrshire:
Comes from Scotland. Its milk
is very rich in butter fat. It
has characteristic lyre-shaped
horns. The bulls are very
large.

Guernsey:
A small breed of cow from the
Channel Islands. It is purely
a dairy breed, and is one of
the most common in Britain.

South Devon:
The largest British breed, with
bulls weighing up to a ton.
Cows give a big yield of rich
milk.

Red Poll:
An East Anglian hornless
breed, good for both milk and
beef.

The Milking Parlour

Cows are milked by machines that imitate the sucking of a calf.
The milk is drawn by suction through tubes into large glass
jars and then piped to a large refrigerated tank where it is
cooled before being taken away in a milk tanker.

Sheep

There are three main types of sheep: long wools, short wools and hill breeds.

The long wools have long glossy fleeces which make very fine cloth, but they often do not make good meat. Wensleydale, Devon, Romney Marsh and Leicester are some of the breeds.

The short wools have clean faces and legs. Their fleeces are good for knitting wools and they are also good for meat. Shropshire, Dorset Down and Suffolk are typical breeds.

Some of the oldest breeds come from the hills, like the Cheviot, the Welsh Mountain and the Scottish Blackface. The Herdwick sheep from Cumberland are believed to have been brought there by the Norsemen well over a thousand years ago. Hill breeds are among the most numerous, as they make equally good meat and wool.

The male sheep are called rams and the females ewes. Most ewes have one or two lambs at a time. Their young are born in the fields early in the spring. The fleeces are sheared in the summer, and twice a year they have to go through a disinfectant bath called a sheep dip, to protect them from infection.

Herdwick sheep

South Down

Scottish Blackface

Leicester

Pigs

Our domestic pigs are descended from the wild ones that roamed the primeval forests of early Britain. They are clean and highly intelligent animals. The male is known as a boar, the female a gilt until she has produced her first litter, after which she is called a sow. There are about a dozen modern breeds. Some are used for bacon, some for pork, others for canned meat or sausages. One of the oldest breeds that you can see is the Wessex Saddleback, which is good for both pork and bacon production. Another old breed is the Gloucester Old Spot. One of the most common is the Large White from Yorkshire, which is used for bacon, as is the Swedish Landrace. Black breeds like the Berkshire and the Large Black are good in warm climates as they do not get sunburn.

Saddleback

Large White

Gloucester Old Spot

Poultry

The jungle fowl which you see above comes from south-east Asia and it is the ancestor of the ordinary domestic chicken. The Romans probably introduced it into Britain along with the pheasant. There are now more than fifty different breeds of chicken. Some are good for egg production, some for meat, and there are breeds that are good for both. Among the laying birds are the Ancona and the Leghorn, while the Dorking and the Old English Game are known as 'table birds'. Dual purpose breeds are the Buff Orpington, Plymouth Rock and the Rhode Island Red. Today, breeds are mostly crossed to produce hybrids.

Once every farmyard had chickens running free, and the cock crowing before dawn was a part of country life. Now chickens are kept in windowless buildings where the light and heat are controlled.

A Plymouth Rock Cockerel

The needs of farming have shaped the landscape that we see around us. Most of Britain is farmed so what landowners and farmers do with the land affects us all. Luckily, most of our farmers are well aware of their responsibility. They have to decide what changes to make so as to gain full advantage of modern technology. These decisions also interest organisations like the National Trust, who protect some of our most beautiful and useful countryside for us. Preservation of some of the traditional features of the landscape may help to keep the land farmed properly.

A case in point is that of hedges, many of which are being 'grubbed out' so as to create larger fields which are easier to plough and cultivate. These hedges, some of them over a

thousand years old, provide protection for the soil from cold and wind. Without this shelter, top-soil can be blown away and the soil damaged. Hedges are also animal corridors providing safe cover for wild life.

There is also good reason to preserve old breeds of domestic livestock, both for historical and scientific purposes. Many of our farm animals are cross-bred, sometimes with old breeds that have particularly favourable characteristics. The Rare Breeds Survival Trust have helped to save many rare species for us, like the brown curly Soay sheep above, an ancient breed that goes back to Neolithic times. Without aid, breeds like Highland cattle will soon disappear for ever.

MARCH

APRIL

SPRING PLANTING
OF BARLEY
POTATOES
VEGETABLES

EARLY GRASS IS
GRAZED BY
COWS

GRASS-CUTTING
FOR SILAGE

MAY

HENS START LAYING

FEBRUARY

A FARMING
CALENDAR

JANUARY

POULTRY READY
FOR CHRISTMAS

DECEMBER

NEWLY
SOWN
WINTER
WHEAT

CUTTING SUGAR
BEET

FIELDS PLOUGHED
FOR NEW CROP

NOVEMBER

OCTOBER

SHEEP SHEARING
IN THE SOUTH
LAMBS SENT TO MARKET

HAYMAKING

OATS

HARVEST OF
WINTER BARLEY
OR OATS.

JUNE

JULY

AUGUST

SEPTEMBER

SOWING GRASS
~ FERTILISER APPLIED ~

HARVEST FOR WHEAT
BARLEY
OATS

HOPS ARE
RIPENING

POTATO
PICKING

SHEEP IN FOLDS
FED ON FODDER

ROOT CROPS STORED
IN CLAMPS

Farm Horses

There are three main British breeds. The Shire from the Midlands is a heavily built animal with a lot of hair flowing beneath the knee and hock, called 'feathering'. This may well be descended from the war horses of the ancient Britons. It was certainly used to carry knights in full armour in the Middle Ages. Then there is the Clydesdale which comes from Scotland and the North, not quite so massive but otherwise rather similar. The third is the Suffolk Punch, illustrated below, less heavily built than the other two, and always a chestnut colour without much mane or feathering.

It is only since the eighteenth century that horses have been used as draught animals. Before that time oxen were used. As farm machinery grew heavier, larger horses were bred to do the pulling, until eventually horses were superseded by tractors. However, horses still continue to be used in some areas to do light carting jobs, where they do less harm to wet soil than heavy tractors. Lighter horses like the Welsh Cob, the Dales Pony and the Highland Garron are used in rough hilly districts.

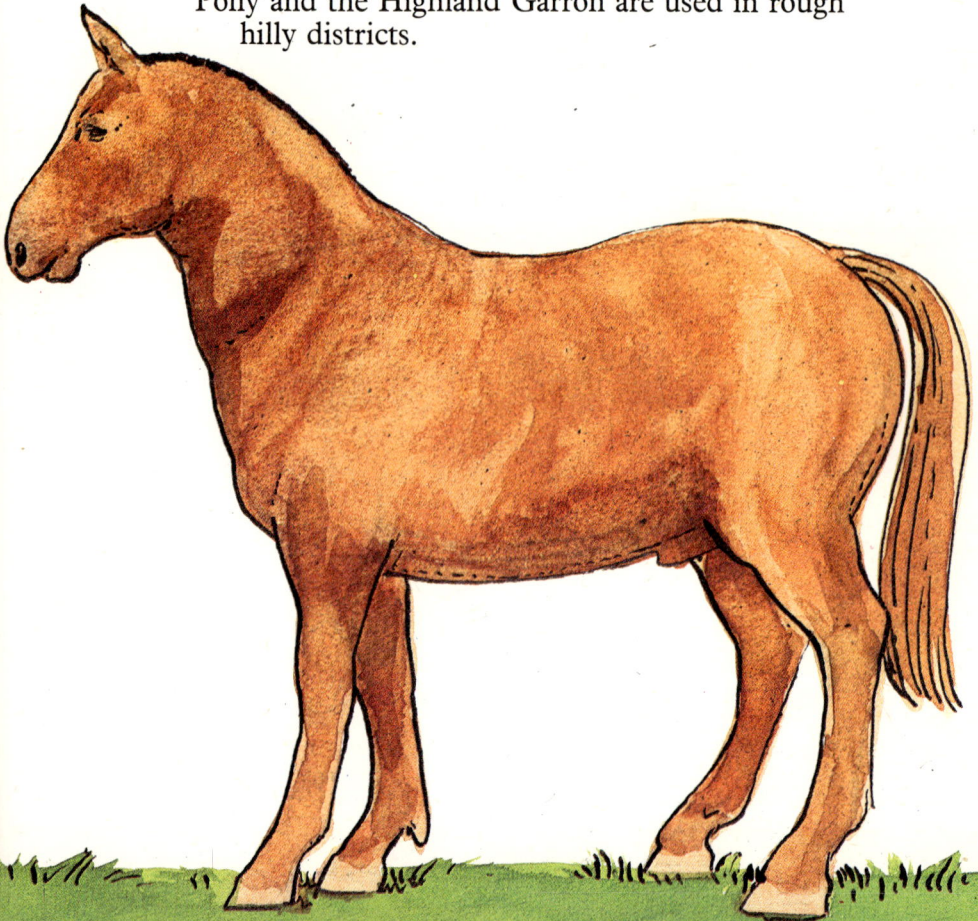